Profiles of the Presidents

GEORGE WASHINGTON

★ ★ ★

Profiles of the Presidents

GEORGE WASHINGTON

by Michael Burgan

Content Adviser: Mary V. Thompson, Research Specialist, Collections Department, Mount Vernon Ladies' Association, Mount Vernon, Virginia

Social Science Adviser: Professor Sherry L. Field, Department of Curriculum and Instruction, College of Education, The University of Texas at Austin

Reading Adviser: Dr. Linda D. Labbo, Department of Reading Education, College of Education, The University of Georgia

Compass Point Books
3722 West 50th Street, #115
Minneapolis, MN 55410

Visit Compass Point Books on the Internet at *www.compasspointbooks.com*
or e-mail your request to *custserv@compasspointbooks.com*

Editors: E. Russell Primm, Emily J. Dolbear, and Melissa McDaniel
Photo Researchers: Svetlana Zhurkina and Jo Miller
Photo Selector: Heidi Schoof
Designer: The Design Lab

Library of Congress Cataloging-in-Publication Data

Burgan, Michael.
   George Washington / by Michael Burgan.
     p. cm. — (Profiles of the presidents)
   Includes bibliographical references and index.
   Summary: A biography of George Washington from his boyhood in Virginia, through his work as a
land surveyor, planter, soldier, and as the president who set a high standard for all who would follow.
   ISBN 0-7565-0204-7
   1. Washington, George, 1732–1799—Juvenile literature. 2. Presidents—United States—
Biography—Juvenile literature. [1. Washington, George, 1732–1799. 2. Presidents.] I. Title. II. Series.
   E312.66 .B87 2002
   973.4'1'092—dc21   2001004735

Table of Contents

★   ★   ★

A Leader in War and Peace

★ ★ ★

In 1775, when the American **colonies** began their fight for independence from Great Britain, they turned to George Washington to lead their army. After the Revolutionary War (1775–1783), the United States tried to create a government that worked well. When leaders met to shape this new government, they made George Washington the president of the meeting. And when their new government finally began, most Americans agreed on who should lead it—George Washington.

Washington was not the best educated of the leaders who shaped America. He was not the wealthiest, either. Many historians say Washington was not even a great general. He sometimes doubted his own talents as a leader. And he would often have gladly traded his fame and power for a quiet farmer's life in Virginia. But every time he was called to serve, he was ready.

◄ Gilbert Stuart's 1796 portrait of George Washington hangs in the historic East Room at the White House. The painting was rescued by First Lady Dolley Madison when British troops set fire to the mansion in 1814.

Washington has often been called the Father of Our Country. His fellow general—Henry "Light-Horse Harry" Lee—said Washington was "first in war, first in peace, and

The face of ▶
George Washington
viewed from the
far left of the
sculpture at
Mount Rushmore
National Monument
in South Dakota

first in the hearts of his countrymen." Thomas Jefferson praised Washington for his courage and honesty: "He was indeed . . . a wise, a good, a great man." Above all, Washington was devoted to the new nation he helped create.

The Young Soldier

★ ★ ★

Like many of America's early leaders, Washington was from Virginia. He was born on February 22, 1732, at Pope's Creek Plantation, his father's farm in eastern Virginia. His father, Augustine, also owned land farther north along the Potomac River. Washington's mother, Mary, was Augustine's second wife.

◄ George Washington Birthplace National Monument in Westmoreland County, Virginia

In 1735, the Washingtons moved to their land along the Potomac, called Little Hunting Creek. Augustine Washington made a living by growing tobacco and by turning raw iron ore into metal. The family was not rich compared to some Virginians, but the Washingtons lived well. In 1738, they moved again. This time they went a bit farther west, to Ferry Farm near Fredericksburg, Virginia.

Lawrence ▲
Washington

When George was six, he met his older brother, Lawrence, for the first time. Lawrence was the son of Augustine's first wife. He had been studying in England when George was born. He and George became good friends. A few years later, Lawrence served in the British army. George's interest in becoming a soldier may have come from Lawrence's war stories.

As a boy, George went to school off and on. Mostly, he studied at home. He also helped on the family farm. And, like most boys in Virginia at that time, he learned how to hunt, fish, and ride horses.

George's father died in 1743, and Lawrence became the head of the family. He gave the farm at Little Hunting Creek a new name. He called it Mount Vernon.

Washington's Mount Vernon home

A few years later, Lawrence became ill. In the fall of 1751, he decided to sail to Barbados, an island in the Caribbean Sea. Lawrence hoped the warm weather there would improve his health. George went with Lawrence on the trip. It was the only trip George ever made outside America.

During the trip, George caught smallpox, a deadly

Bathsheba Beach ▶
on the island of
Barbados

Robert Dinwiddie
was lieutenant
governor of Virginia
from 1751 to 1758. ▼

disease. He recovered, but the illness left marks on his face that never went away. The trip did not help Lawrence's health, either. He died in 1752, at the age of thirty-four.

At the time of his death, Lawrence had been in charge of Virginia's **militia**. Although George had never been a soldier, he hoped to take over his brother's post. Robert Dinwiddie, the lieutenant governor of Virginia, decided to split the colony into four districts. Each would have its own militia leader. George was put in charge of the southern district. In December 1752, he became Major George Washington.

Just shy of his twenty-first birthday, Washington was already a big man. He had grown to over 6 feet (182 centimeters) tall, with long arms and legs and a strong body. He may not have known much about war, but he looked like a leader.

Washington did not have to wait long for his first military experience. Great Britain and France were fighting for control of North America. France owned most of eastern Canada as well as the land along the Mississippi River. Great Britain had its thirteen American colonies along the East Coast and Nova Scotia, part of eastern Canada. Both France and Great Britain tried to control land along the Ohio River. Both also tried to get Indian tribes to fight along with them.

Early in 1753, the French built a fort on land claimed by Great Britain. Lieutenant Governor Dinwiddie wrote a letter to the French, ordering them to leave British land. Washington offered to deliver the letter. He traveled through Native American lands, where he met an Indian chief named Half King. The chief and some of his men

Washington ▲
traveled through
frontier territory
to deliver Lt. Gov-
ernor Dinwiddie's
letter of warning
to the French.

traveled with Washington. A few weeks later, Washington
delivered Dinwiddie's letter.

On January 16, 1754, Washington returned with the
reply from the French—they would not leave the Ohio
country. Washington also reported that the French were
starting to build more forts. The risk of war grew.

Within a few months, Washington was back in Ohio

country. He was now a lieutenant colonel, and he led more than 100 troops. On the night of May 27, Washington and some of his soldiers discovered a French camp. With the help of Half King and his men, Washington's troops attacked the French, killing ten men and capturing twenty-two. Later, Washington was quoted as saying, "I heard the bullets whistle, and, believe me, there is something charming in the sound."

▲ *Washington's attack on the French*

This attack is sometimes called the first battle of the French and Indian War (1754–1763). For the next few years, the French and British fought each other, with Indians helping both sides.

After the war began, Washington was **promoted** to colonel. One of his first tasks was to build a fort in western Pennsylvania. He named it Fort Necessity. The French and

Washington considering the surrender of Fort Necessity, the only surrender of his military career.

their Indian supporters attacked on July 3, 1754. A heavy rain soaked the Americans' **gunpowder** so that their guns wouldn't work, and Washington was forced to give up.

In July 1755, Washington and other Virginians marched with the British toward Fort Duquesne, in what is now Pittsburgh, Pennsylvania. They planned to take the fort from French and Indian forces and drive them out of the upper Ohio Valley.

Along the way, they were suddenly attacked. The British soldiers panicked, but the Virginians fought well.

The expedition's leader, British General Edward Braddock, was badly wounded and soon died of his injuries. Washington rallied the soldiers and later wrote, "I luckily escaped [without] a Wound tho' I had four bullets thro' my coat & two Horses shot under me."

After this defeat, Washington returned to Virginia. He took command of the colony's defense in the west. He held that job until 1758. By then, the British were winning the war, and Washington was ready to settle down. He went home to Mount Vernon, which he now owned.

▲ *General Braddock was killed in an ambush on the way to Fort Duquesne, now known as the Battle of Monongahela.*

Planter and Politician

★ ★ ★

Early in 1759, Washington married Martha Dandridge Custis. Her first husband had died and left her thousands of acres of land. She also had two children, Jackie and Patsy. Washington became a loving stepfather. He and Martha never had children of their own.

The wedding ▶ of George Washington and Martha Dandridge Custis

At Mount Vernon, Washington lived the normal life of a Virginia **plantation** owner. He worked hard to grow crops, including tobacco, wheat, and flax. He also enjoyed going to parties with other **planters** and their wives. Washington often invited people to Mount Vernon, and he remained a friendly host the rest of his life.

Like most plantation owners in Virginia, Washington also owned slaves. Later in life, Washington hoped for an end to slavery and decided not to buy or sell any more slaves. But he always relied on slaves to take care of his

Washington and his step-grandchildren are shown with slaves in the fields at Mount Vernon.

This reconstruction ▶
of the capitol
of the Virginia
colony can be
visited at Colonial
Williamsburg.

house and plantation. By the time he died, more than 300 slaves worked at Mount Vernon. In his will, Washington arranged to free all the slaves he owned—123 people.

After leaving the military, Washington also became involved in politics. In 1758, he was elected to the **House of Burgesses,** the part of the Virginia government that made laws. Washington did not speak out much during his early years in the House of Burgesses. But starting in 1765, he and other American politicians grew upset over some of Great Britain's actions.

That year, the British **Parliament** passed the Stamp Act. This law placed a tax on all paper goods used in the American colonies. The British needed to raise money after fighting the French and Indian War.

When the Stamp Act was passed, some Americans began to complain about "taxation without representation." The American colonists were British citizens. They believed that Britain could not tax them unless they were allowed to send representatives to Parliament. But the British said they could tax the Americans even if the colonists did not have representatives in Parliament.

Americans in all the colonies protested the Stamp Act. Finally, Parliament removed the tax. But the British continued to add new taxes. In 1769, Washington and the other members of the House of Burgesses said they were the only people who had the right to tax Virginia. Britain ignored them.

Over the next few years, relations between America and Britain worsened. In 1773, some people in Boston, Massachusetts, decided to protest a tax on tea. One night the colonists, dressed as American Indians, raided British ships and threw hundreds of crates of tea into the harbor.

The colonists ▶ protested the Stamp Act by rioting and burning printed materials.

Washington did not support this event, which became known as the Boston Tea Party. But he thought the British reaction was too harsh. British authorities closed Boston Harbor and sent more soldiers to the city. They also took away power from local governments. More Americans were now ready to take stronger actions against the British.

▲ *The Boston Tea Party*

The Commander in Chief

★ ★ ★

In September 1774, representatives from the American colonies met in Philadelphia, Pennsylvania. At this First Continental Congress, the leaders discussed what to do next. Washington represented Virginia at the meeting. He also went to the Second Continental Congress, in May 1775. By then, the colonies and Britain were at war.

No one knows who fired the first shot at the Battle of Lexington, the start of the Revolutionary War (1775–1783).

Massachusetts soldiers and British troops had clashed in the towns of Lexington and Concord.

The Continental Congress decided to create an army. Soldiers from all the colonies would help fight the British in Massachusetts. Washington was named commander in chief of this new Continental army. Washington told Congress, "I do not think myself equal to the Command I am honoured with." Still, he took the job. Washington did

▲ George Washington was appointed commander in chief of the Continental army.

British ships in Boston Harbor, drawn by famous patriot Paul Revere for the North American Almanack

not get paid for commanding the Continental army. He asked only that Congress pay him back for his expenses.

Meanwhile, in Boston, American forces had surrounded the British troops. The British, however, had powerful ships in the harbor. And they had better weapons than the Americans did. In addition, the American troops were poorly trained. Washington had trouble getting along with the soldiers from the Northeast. In one letter, he called the troops "an exceeding dirty and nasty people." Word leaked out that the general did not think much of these men. Afterward, he tried to keep such opinions to himself.

As the year went on, Washington faced another problem. His soldiers had agreed to serve for a certain amount of time, and then they expected to go home. By early 1776, about half of Washington's soldiers had already served their time. So one of the general's main jobs during the Revolutionary War was finding enough soldiers.

By March 1776, Washington had built up his defenses. This convinced the British they could not defeat the Americans at Boston, so they left the city. Congress gave Washington a gold medal for his success—but the war had just begun.

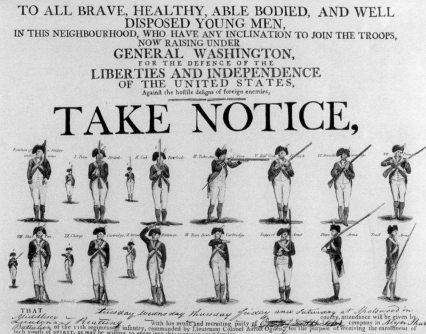

A recruiting poster from the Revolutionary War (1775-1783)

The signing of
the Declaration
of Independence,
as painted by
John Trumbull

Washington and his men headed for New York City,
figuring the British would attack there next. At the same
time, American troops were fighting—and losing—in
Canada. When the British reached New York, they beat
the Continental army in some battles in and around the
city. By December, the Americans had been forced back
into New Jersey, and then into Pennsylvania.

By now, all Americans knew what was at stake in the
war. In July, Congress had approved the Declaration of
Independence. A victory by Washington and his troops
would give America this independence. A loss meant

American leaders would be arrested as **traitors** to Great Britain.

Washington knew he needed to win a battle to give Americans hope. That victory came on December 26, 1776, when Washington launched a surprise attack. Under cover of darkness, Washington and his men crossed the Delaware River from Pennsylvania into New Jersey. There they attacked a group of Hessians—German soldiers who were fighting for the British. A week later, the Americans won another battle in the area. In 1777, however, Washington suffered a bad loss at Brandywine,

▲ *Emanuel Gottlieb Leutze's famous painting,* Washington Crossing the Delaware

These Continental ▲ soldiers' cabins have been reconstructed at the site of Washington's winter camp–Valley Forge National Park, Pennsylvania.

Pennsylvania. The British took control of Philadelphia, which was serving as the U.S. capital.

In December, Washington's army settled in at Valley Forge, Pennsylvania. The cold winter of 1777–1778 was one of the worst times of the war for Washington. He did not have enough food for the soldiers. Most wore rags and had neither shoes nor blankets. Washington wrote letters to Congress trying to get more supplies, but little help came. Finally, by February, some food reached the camp.

During that brutal winter, however, the Americans trained hard. They would be ready to fight when spring came.

By then, the Americans had a new friend—France. The French were going to send money and troops to help the United States fight the British. The French help came slowly, though. In the meantime, Washington used his troops to keep the British in New York. In the South, the British won victories in South Carolina, Virginia, and Georgia. But in the Ohio Valley, the Americans took control of several British forts.

In 1781, Washington faked an attack on New York and marched to Virginia. About 5,000 French troops were with him, and more were on their way by ship. On September 28, the U.S. and French troops met the British at

Washington and Lafayette at Valley Forge: The young Marquis de Lafayette came from France to volunteer in the American fight for independence. He became a member of Washington's staff, and remained a close friend until Washington's death.

Washington ▶
Before Yorktown
by famous
American painter
Rembrandt Peale

Yorktown. Washington fired the first cannon shot. Behind the British troops, French ships blocked any chance of escape by sea. On October 19, British general Charles Lord Cornwallis gave up. Soon after, Britain realized it could not defeat the Americans. The United States won its freedom, and George Washington became its first national hero.

Creating a Government

★ ★ ★

The fighting was over, but Washington's troops were not happy. Congress still owed them money. Some of his men said that Washington should become king and take over the government. Washington was shocked by this idea.

The war officially ended in September 1783. In June 1783, Washington announced his plans to retire from the

◄ General George Washington says good-bye to his officers at Fraunces Tavern in New York City at the end of the Revolutionary War.

military. He also offered some advice. The new nation, Washington said, needed a strong national government to survive. The states needed to work together and do what was best for the nation as a whole.

Washington had seen how hard it was to build a national army. Building a country would be at least as hard. In 1781, the states had approved the Articles of Confederation. This document created America's first national government, but that government was weak. Some states did not want to give up their own powers. They sometimes acted like thirteen separate nations, and not united states. Washington already saw the problems this would create in the future.

Over time, more and more Americans spoke out against the Articles of Confederation. They believed the United States needed a stronger national government. Although Washington believed this, too, he mostly stayed out of politics. He returned to Mount Vernon and became a planter again. By 1786, however, the country seemed to be heading for trouble.

In some states, farmers faced losing their land because they could not pay their taxes. In Massachusetts, people protested this by starting a **rebellion.** Daniel Shays, a

An army of local militiamen successfully defended the federal arsenal in Springfield, Massachusetts, against Shays's rebels on January 25, 1787.

former army captain, led the rebels. They tried to take weapons stored in Springfield. The attack failed, but "Shays's Rebellion" worried some Americans. They

▲ *George Washington leading the Constitutional Convention*

believed a strong national government might have kept the rebellion from happening.

In May 1787, leaders from around the nation met in Philadelphia to change the Articles of Confederation. At this meeting, they wrote the **Constitution.** This document spelled out the form of the new government. Washington was asked to represent Virginia at this Constitutional **Convention.** At first Washington did not want to go. But others convinced him he could help make sure the new government was strong enough to survive.

The other representatives at the convention elected Washington president of the convention. He did not take part in the debates that shaped the Constitution, though. In private, he wrote that the men who were against a strong government "are, in my opinion, narrow-minded politicians."

James Monroe became the fifth president of the United States in 1817.

Although Washington did not say much at the convention, he played an important role. The other delegates there respected him. They also knew how much he wanted a more powerful government. James Monroe, another Virginian, wrote, "Be assured, his influence carried this government."

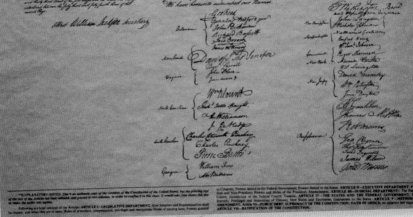

The type of government created in Philadelphia is still in power today. It has three parts, or branches. The legislature—or Congress—has two separate houses, with representatives sent by the states. This is the branch that makes laws. The executive branch, led by the president, carries out these laws. The third branch is the judiciary. Its judges make sure the laws are carried out fairly.

The states began considering the Constitution in late 1787. By June 1788, enough states had approved the Constitution to put the new government in place. When Washington heard the news, he wrote, "No one can rejoice more than I do."

When people began talking about who might be the first president, one name came up more than any other— George Washington. Everyone knew that he was honest and had served his country well. With Washington as president, Americans could believe that the new government would be fair.

The First President

★   ★   ★

In February 1789, representatives from each state met to choose the president. Washington won every vote. In April, he left for New York City, which was then the nation's capital. Along the road, people came out to cheer their new leader.

George Washington ▶
receiving news of his
election to the
presidency

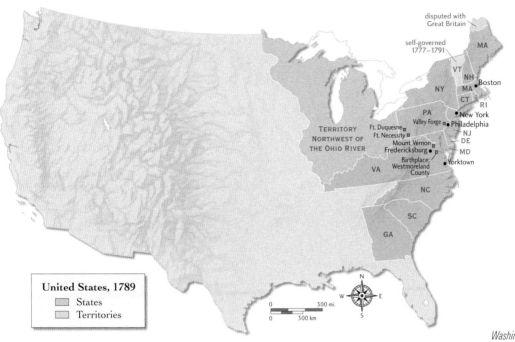

United States, 1789
  States
  Territories

disputed with
Great Britain

self-governed
1777–1791

MA

VT
NH
NY   MA   • Boston
CT
RI
PA   • New York
Valley Forge   • Philadelphia
NJ
DE

TERRITORY   Ft. Duquesne
NORTHWEST OF   Ft. Necessity
THE OHIO RIVER   Mount Vernon   MD
Fredericksburg
Birthplace: • Yorktown
VA   Westmoreland
County

NC

SC

GA

N
W   E
S

0   300 mi.
0   300 km

*Washington's letter
accepting the
▾ presidency*

On April 30, Washington was sworn in as the first president of the United States. In his first speech, Washington asked for God's blessing on the new nation. He also talked about the "experiment" America was beginning with its new government. One senator who heard the speech said

The inauguration ▶ of George Washington as first president of the United States took place on the balcony of Federal Hall in New York City.

Washington seemed nervous or embarrassed: "He trembled, and several times could scarce make out to read."

Washington knew how important his role was. He was not only leading the country now, but his actions would also influence how future presidents acted. He asked Vice President John Adams for suggestions. He also turned to Alexander Hamilton, who had been his aide during the Revolutionary War. Hamilton would become one of Washington's most trusted advisers.

One of Washington's first jobs was to choose leaders for the various government departments. Hamilton became secretary of the treasury. Washington named Thomas Jefferson as secretary of state, to handle foreign affairs. Henry Knox was secretary of war. The nation's top lawyer, the attorney general, was Edmund Randolph. And John Jay became the first chief justice of the U.S. Supreme Court.

The first presidential cabinet (from left): Henry Knox, Thomas Jefferson, Edmund Randolph, and Alexander Hamilton

The new government faced many important issues. The country owed money that had to be repaid. Hamilton was in charge of using taxes to pay off this debt. He also wanted to help industry and trade. Others, such as Jefferson, thought the country should rely more on farming.

Jefferson and Hamilton disagreed on many issues, and they became the leaders of the country's first national political parties. Hamilton and others who supported a strong national government were called Federalists. Jefferson and his supporters were called Republicans. The Republicans wanted to limit the government's power. Washington tended to be a Federalist, but he often avoided taking sides. He let Congress do its job of making the laws. Today, presidents tend to be more involved in suggesting new laws and making sure they are passed.

Jefferson and Hamilton also disagreed on foreign policy. Hamilton wanted good relations with Great Britain. Jefferson supported France. These two countries, along with Spain, still controlled parts of North America. They also sometimes clashed in Europe. Washington wanted the United States to stay out of any war between European nations.

Alexander Hamilton, ▲
Washington's friend
and trusted adviser

Thomas Jefferson ▶
became the third
president of the
United States in
1801, after serving
as vice president
under John Adams.

Despite their differences, Hamilton and Jefferson agreed on one thing—Washington should serve as president for another four years. In 1793, once again, Washington received every vote. His second term, however, was not as easy as his first.

The United States was being dragged into the struggle between Britain and France. These two countries were now at war. Washington said America would not take sides during the war. But over time, tensions rose between the United States and the two warring countries.

A French official tried to convince the Americans to fight for France. This was illegal under Washington's order that the United States not take sides. The French action turned many Americans against France. Later, British warships began capturing

U.S. ships carrying goods. Some Americans feared that the United States and Britain would go to war. John Jay eventually drafted a treaty that improved relations between the two countries.

▲ *John Jay was the first chief justice of the U.S. Supreme Court.*

Illegal whiskey ▲
was made
in hidden
distillation
equipment
called stills.

In 1794, Washington faced trouble at home. Farmers in western Pennsylvania did not want to pay a tax on whiskey. They made this liquor from their own corn and wheat. When state officials tried to force the farmers to pay taxes, riots broke out. Washington sent in about 13,000 troops to end the Whiskey Rebellion. In doing this, he made it clear that the government had the right to collect the tax.

Reaching the End

★ ★ ★

In 1796, Americans wondered if Washington would seek a third term as president. At that time, the Constitution had not set a limit on how long a president could serve. (Today, the limit is two terms.) But in September 1796, Washington gave his last speech as president. In it, Washington gave thanks "to my beloved country for the

◄ George Washington making the rounds of his Mount Vernon farm.

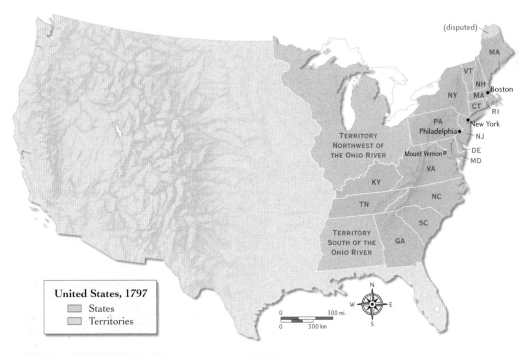

United States, 1797
  States
  Territories

many honors it has [given] me." And once again, Washington stressed the great things all Americans shared. "You have in a common cause fought and triumphed together," he said. "The independence and liberty you possess are the work of . . . joint efforts; of common dangers, sufferings and successes."

In March 1797, Washington returned to his beloved Mount Vernon. Once again, he became a farmer. He also remained interested in politics and even considered serving his country one last time. In 1798, the United States seemed close to war with France. Some people asked if

◄ Washington lies on his deathbed while friends and family gather to say good-bye.

▼ According to legend, young George admits to his father that he chopped down a cherry tree.

Washington would lead the military. Washington said he would, but the war never came.

Washington remained active at Mount Vernon until the end of his life. Just a few days before he died, he spent hours riding around the farm. The next day, he had a sore throat and went to bed. On December 14, 1799, he died peacefully in his bedroom.

After his death, Washington became an even greater American hero. Some people created legends about him. One popular story was that as a boy he had chopped down a cherry tree. He then told his father he had done it, because he could not tell a lie. That story was not true. Still, to some Americans, George Washington seemed like the perfect person—someone who had never done anything wrong.

George Washington was not perfect, of course. Even people who admired his strengths knew he had weaknesses, too. But Washington stood for many things that were important to America. He was ready to fight for freedom. He loved his country and wanted it to be strong. He took command in difficult times. Washington set high standards for other U.S. presidents to follow.

The Washington ▶
Monument in
Washington, D.C.

GLOSSARY

★ ★ ★

colonies—territories settled by people from another country and ruled by that country

Constitution—a written document explaining the basic laws of the United States

convention—a meeting held for a special purpose

gunpowder—a powder that explodes easily; used in guns and firearms

House of Burgesses—the legislature of the Virginia colony

militia—an army of part-time soldiers

Parliament—the part of the British government that makes laws

plantation—a large farm

planters—people who own plantations

promoted—given a higher rank

rebellion—an armed uprising against the government

traitors—people who betray their own country

GEORGE WASHINGTON'S LIFE AT A GLANCE

★ ★ ★

PERSONAL

Nickname:	Father of Our Country
Born:	February 22, 1732
Birthplace:	Pope's Creek Plantation, Westmoreland County, Virginia
Father's name:	Augustine Washington
Mother's name:	Mary Ball Washington
Education:	Seven or eight years in Fredericksburg, Virginia
Wife's name:	Martha Dandridge Custis
Married:	January 6, 1759
Children:	None
Died:	December 14, 1799, at Mount Vernon
Buried:	Mount Vernon

PUBLIC

Occupation before presidency:	Surveyor, plantation manager, plantation owner
Occupation after presidency:	Plantation owner
Military service:	Virginia militia during the French and Indian War; commander in chief of the Continental army
Other government positions:	Member of the House of Burgesses; member of the First and Second Continental Congresses; delegate for Virginia to the Constitutional Convention; president of the Constitutional Convention
Political party:	None
Vice president:	John Adams
Dates in office:	April 30, 1789–March 3, 1797
Presidential opponents:	None
Number of votes (Electoral College):	(69 of 69, 132 of 132)

George Washington's Cabinet

Secretary of state:
John Jay
(1789–1790)
Thomas Jefferson
(1790–1793)
Edmund Randolph
(1794–1795)
Timothy Pickering
(1795–1797)

Secretary of the treasury:
Alexander Hamilton
(1789–1795)
Oliver Wolcott Jr.
(1795–1797)

Secretary of war:
Henry Knox
(1789–1794)
Timothy Pickering
(1795–1796)
James McHenry
(1796–1797)

Attorney general:
Edmund Randolph
(1790–1794)
William Bradford
(1794–1795)
Charles Lee
(1795–1797)

GEORGE WASHINGTON'S LIFE AND TIMES

★ ★ ★

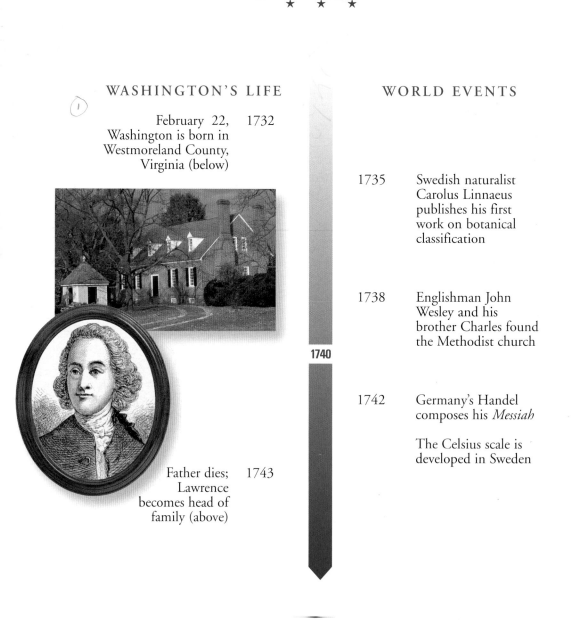

WASHINGTON'S LIFE

February 22, 1732
Washington is born in
Westmoreland County,
Virginia (below)

Father dies; 1743
Lawrence
becomes head of
family (above)

WORLD EVENTS

1735 Swedish naturalist
Carolus Linnaeus
publishes his first
work on botanical
classification

1738 Englishman John
Wesley and his
brother Charles found
the Methodist church

1740

1742 Germany's Handel
composes his *Messiah*

The Celsius scale is
developed in Sweden

WASHINGTON'S LIFE

1750

Joins the Virginia militia; given command of the southern district — 1753

Washington is commissioned a lieutenant colonel in the Virginia militia and fights in the French and Indian War (below) — 1754

Is elected to the Virginia House of Burgesses — 1758

WORLD EVENTS

1749 — German writer Johann Wolfgang Goethe is born

1752 — Benjamin Franklin performs his famous kite experiment (right)

1756– 1763 — The Seven Years' War, known in America as the French and Indian War, is fought (below); Britain defeats France

WASHINGTON'S LIFE		WORLD EVENTS	
Marries Martha Custis (below)	1759	1759	Author Voltaire of France writes his brilliant tale *Candide*
			The British Museum opens in London
	1760		
		1762	Catherine the Great becomes empress of Russia and rules for thirty-four years
		1769	British explorer Captain James Cook reaches New Zealand
	1770	1770	Five die in a street clash that becomes known as the Boston Massacre (below)
Represents Virginia at the First Continental Congress	1774		
Serves as a Virginia delegate to the Second Continental Congress in Philadelphia	1775		
Becomes commander in chief of the Continental army (above)			

WASHINGTON'S LIFE

Leads troops across the   1776
Delaware River in a
successful attack
(right)

Trains troops during   1777–
the harsh winter at   1778
Valley Forge (below)

His troops defeat   1781
British general
Charles Cornwallis at
Yorktown, Virginia
(below)

WORLD EVENTS

1777   Vermont is the first
former colony to ban
slavery

1779   Jan Ingenhousz of the
Netherlands discovers
that plants release
oxygen when exposed
to sunlight

1780

1783   American author
Washington Irving
is born

★

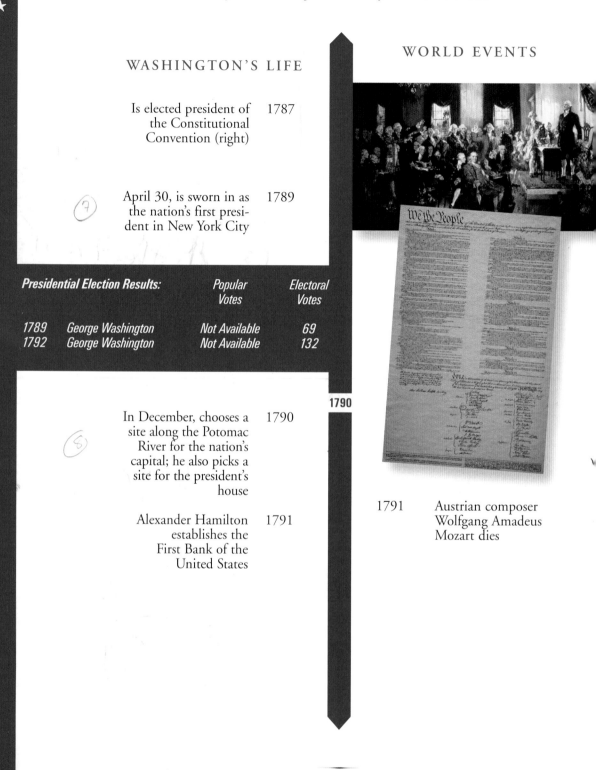

WASHINGTON'S LIFE

WORLD EVENTS

Is elected president of the Constitutional Convention (right) — 1787

April 30, is sworn in as the nation's first president in New York City — 1789

⑦

Presidential Election Results:		Popular Votes	Electoral Votes
1789	George Washington	Not Available	69
1792	George Washington	Not Available	132

1790

In December, chooses a site along the Potomac River for the nation's capital; he also picks a site for the president's house — 1790

⑧

Alexander Hamilton establishes the First Bank of the United States — 1791

1791 — Austrian composer Wolfgang Amadeus Mozart dies

WASHINGTON'S LIFE

1792 In October, the first cornerstone for the president's house is laid

Is reelected president

1794 Sends 13,000 soldiers to crush the Whiskey Rebellion in Pennsylvania (right)

1799 December 14, dies at Mount Vernon (below) of a throat infection

WORLD EVENTS

1792 The dollar currency is introduced to America

1799 Napoléon Bonaparte (below) takes control of France

1800

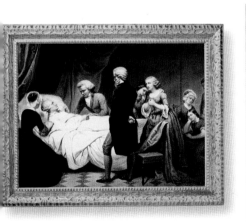

UNDERSTANDING GEORGE WASHINGTON AND HIS PRESIDENCY

★ ★ ★

IN THE LIBRARY

Collier, Christopher. *Building a New Nation: The Federalist Era, 1789-1801.* New York: Benchmark Books, 1999.

Grote, JoAnn A. *The American Revolution.* Broomall, Penn.: Chelsea House, 1999.

Marrin, Albert. *George Washington & the Founding of a Nation.* New York: Dutton Children's Books, 2001.

Rosenburg, John M. *First in War: George Washington in the American Revolution.* Brookfield, Conn.: Millbrook Press, 1998.

Simon, Charnan. *Martha Dandridge Custis Washington.* Danbury, Conn.: Children's Press, 2000.

ON THE WEB

The History Place: Washington Photo Gallery
*http://www.historyplace.com/unitedstates/
revolution/wash-pix/gallery.htm*
For pictures about Washington's life and presidency

Internet Public Library—George Washington
http://www.ipl.org/ref/POTUS/gwashington.html
For more information about Washington's presidency, as well as trivia about his presidency

George Washington Quiz
http://www.osv.org/gw/wquiz2.htm
For a fun quiz about George Washington's life and the myths about him

George Washington
http://www.ushistory.org/valleyforge/washington/
For activities and information about Washington

WASHINGTON HISTORIC SITES ACROSS THE COUNTRY

George Washington Birthplace National Monument
1732 Pope's Creek Plantation
Washington's Birthplace, VA 22443-5115
804/224-1732
To view the house where Washington was born

Mount Vernon— Washington's Home
P.O. Box 110
Mount Vernon, VA 22121
703/780-2000
To visit George Washington's house and gardens

Valley Forge National Historic Park
P.O. Box 953
Valley Forge, PA 19482-0953
610/783-1077
To visit the site where the Continental army spent a brutal winter

Washington Monument
900 Ohio Drive, S.W.
Washington, DC 20024-2000
202/426-6841
To see the landmark tribute to the first president of the United States

THE U.S. PRESIDENTS
(Years in Office)

★ ★ ★

1. **George Washington**
(March 4, 1789–March 3, 1797)
2. **John Adams**
(March 4, 1797–March 3, 1801)
3. **Thomas Jefferson**
(March 4, 1801–March 3, 1809)
4. **James Madison**
(March 4, 1809–March 3, 1817)
5. **James Monroe**
(March 4, 1817–March 3, 1825)
6. **John Quincy Adams**
(March 4, 1825–March 3, 1829)
7. **Andrew Jackson**
(March 4, 1829–March 3, 1837)
8. **Martin Van Buren**
(March 4, 1837–March 3, 1841)
9. **William Henry Harrison**
(March 6, 1841–April 4, 1841)
10. **John Tyler**
(April 6, 1841–March 3, 1845)
11. **James K. Polk**
(March 4, 1845–March 3, 1849)
12. **Zachary Taylor**
(March 5, 1849–July 9, 1850)
13. **Millard Fillmore**
(July 10, 1850–March 3, 1853)
14. **Franklin Pierce**
(March 4, 1853–March 3, 1857)
15. **James Buchanan**
(March 4, 1857–March 3, 1861)
16. **Abraham Lincoln**
(March 4, 1861–April 15, 1865)
17. **Andrew Johnson**
(April 15, 1865–March 3, 1869)

18. **Ulysses S. Grant**
(March 4, 1869–March 3, 1877)
19. **Rutherford B. Hayes**
(March 4, 1877–March 3, 1881)
20. **James Garfield**
(March 4, 1881–Sept 19, 1881)
21. **Chester Arthur**
(Sept 20, 1881–March 3, 1885)
22. **Grover Cleveland**
(March 4, 1885–March 3, 1889)
23. **Benjamin Harrison**
(March 4, 1889–March 3, 1893)
24. **Grover Cleveland**
(March 4, 1893–March 3, 1897)
25. **William McKinley**
(March 4, 1897–September 14, 1901)
26. **Theodore Roosevelt**
(September 14, 1901–March 3, 1909)
27. **William Howard Taft**
(March 4, 1909–March 3, 1913)
28. **Woodrow Wilson**
(March 4, 1913–March 3, 1921)
29. **Warren G. Harding**
(March 4, 1921–August 2, 1923)
30. **Calvin Coolidge**
(August 3, 1923–March 3, 1929)
31. **Herbert Hoover**
(March 4, 1929–March 3, 1933)
32. **Franklin D. Roosevelt**
(March 4, 1933–April 12, 1945)

33. **Harry S. Truman**
(April 12, 1945–January 20, 1953)
34. **Dwight D. Eisenhower**
(January 20, 1953–January 20, 1961)
35. **John F. Kennedy**
(January 20, 1961–November 22, 1963)
36. **Lyndon B. Johnson**
(November 22, 1963–January 20, 1969)
37. **Richard M. Nixon**
(January 20, 1969–August 9, 1974)
38. **Gerald R. Ford**
(August 9, 1974–January 20, 1977)
39. **James Earl Carter**
(January 20, 1977–January 20, 1981)
40. **Ronald Reagan**
(January 20, 1981–January 20, 1989)
41. **George H. W. Bush**
(January 20, 1989–January 20, 1993)
42. **William Jefferson Clinton**
(January 20, 1993–January 20, 2001)
43. **George W. Bush**
(January 20, 2001–)

INDEX

★ ★ ★

ABOUT THE AUTHOR

Michael Burgan is a freelance writer of books for children and adults. A history graduate of the University of Connecticut, he has written more than thirty fiction and nonfiction children's books for various publishers. For adult audiences, he has written news articles, essays, and plays. Michael Burgan is a recipient of an Edpress Award and belongs to the Society of Children's Book Writers and Illustrators.